Ladybird  Readers

Wild Animals

Series Editor: Sorrel Pitts
Text adapted by Sorrel Pitts
Illustrated by Natalie Hinrichsen

LADYBIRD BOOKS

UK | USA | Canada | Ireland | Australia
India | New Zealand | South Africa

Ladybird Books is part of the Penguin Random House group of companies
whose addresses can be found at global.penguinrandomhouse.com.
www.penguin.co.uk   www.puffin.co.uk   www.ladybird.com

First published 2016
006
Copyright © Ladybird Books Ltd, 2016

The moral rights of the author and illustrator have been asserted.

Printed in China

A CIP catalogue record for this book is available from the British Library

ISBN: 978–0–241–25445–5

Wild Animals

Contents

Picture words

 cheetah

 desert

 dolphin

 elephant

 fennec fox

 gibbon

 jungle

 parrot

 plains

 polar bear

 scorpion

 shark

Wild animals

Wild animals do not live with people. They do not live on farms.

Some wild animals live together in large groups. Some wild animals live in small families.

These are all wild animals.

Elephants

There are groups of
elephants on the plains.

plains

elephant

calf

Elephant calves live in big groups with their mothers, brothers, and sisters.

An elephant is a big, big animal.

Cheetahs

Cheetahs live on the plains.

Cheetah cubs live with
their mother and their
brothers and sisters.

cubs

A mother cheetah and her cubs.

Cheetahs are big animals.
They can run very fast.

cheetah

Gibbons

There are many gibbons in the jungle.

Gibbons live in family groups.

mother gibbon

jungle

Gibbons go from tree to tree.

Parrots

All these parrots live in the jungle.

Some parrots live in little groups. Some parrots live in big groups.

Where is the big group of parrots?

Parrots go from tree to tree.

Fennec foxes

This wild animal is a fennec fox.

It lives in the desert in a family group.

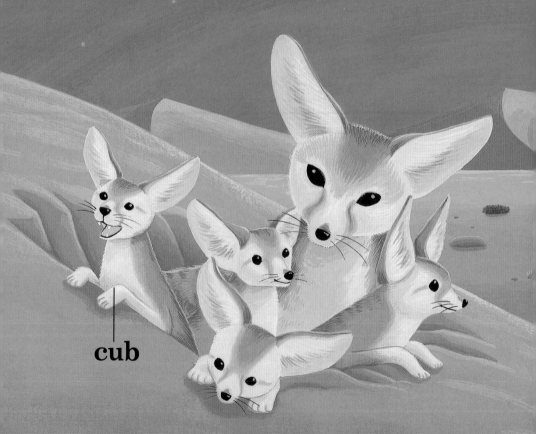

cub

The fennec fox is not a big animal.

All the group help
the fennec fox cubs.

fennec fox ——

desert

Scorpions

There are many scorpions in the desert.

A mother helps her children.

children

Can you see the scorpion children?

scorpion

Polar bears

This is a polar bear. It lives in the Arctic.

polar bear

A polar bear cub lives with his mother and his brother or sister.

Arctic

cub

These polar bears live in the Arctic.

Dolphins

There are many dolphins in the sea.

These dolphins and their calves live in family groups.

calf   dolphin

Dolphins are big sea animals.

Sharks

There are a lot of
sharks in the sea.

Some are big and
some are little.

Many sharks are big animals!

This shark is a little animal.

Activities

The key below describes the skills practiced in each activity.

✏️ Spelling and writing

📖 Reading

💬 Speaking

❓ Critical thinking

🏅 Preparation for the Cambridge Young Learners Exams

1 **Look and read.**
Put a or a in the box.

1  This is an elephant with two calves.

2  This is a fennec fox.

3  This is a gibbon.

4  These are parrots.

5  This is a shark.

2 **Look and read.**
Write yes or no. 📖 ✏️ ✴️

Wild animals

Wild animals do not live with people. They do not live on farms.

Some wild animals live together in large groups. Some wild animals live in small families.

These are all wild animals.

8

9

1 Some wild animals live together in groups. ....yes.............

2 Some wild animals live on farms. ....

3 Some wild animals never live in large groups. ....

4 Some wild animals live in small families. ....

3 **Work with a friend.**
Talk about the two pictures.
How are they different? 💬

a

Parrots

All these parrots live in
the jungle.

Some parrots live in little
groups. Some parrots live
in big groups.

Where is the big group of parrots?

16

b

Parrots go from tree to tree.

17

Example:

> In picture a,
> there is a little
> group of parrots.

> In picture b,
> there is a big
> group of parrots.

4 Find the words.

c	u	b	o	s	c
n	x	u	y	c	a
o	g	o	x	o	l
s	r	n	k	r	v
h	o	i	q	p	e
a	u	e	n	i	s
r	p	q	w	o	b
k	s	u	a	n	k

cub

calves

groups

scorpion

shark

5 **Read the text. Choose a word from the box. Write the correct word next to numbers 1—5.**

> cub   calves   family
> mothers   wild

Elephants are [1] _wild_

animals. Some wild animals live

in [2] _____ groups. Elephant

[3] _____ live in big groups

with their brothers and sisters.

Their [4] _____ help them, too.

A polar bear [5] _____ lives with

his mother and brother or sister.

6 **Circle the correct word.**

1 Elephant calves live with their
(**mothers**) / **fathers**.

2 A **cheetah** / **parrot** can run
very fast.

3 Parrots can **fly** / **swim**.

4 Fennec foxes live in
hot / **cold** places.

5 Scorpion mothers have
two or three / **many** little
scorpion children.

7 Look at the pictures. One picture
is different. How is it different?
Tell your teacher. ○

Example:

Picture d is different
because the animal
does not live in the sea.

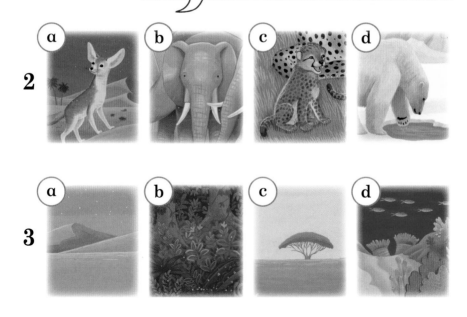

8 **Look and read.**
Write the answers.

1 Which animals have got big ears?

Elephants have got big ears.

2 Which animals have got long ears?

_____

3 Which big animals are white?

_____

4 Which big animals live in the sea?

_____

9 Ask and answer the questions with a friend.

1 Do dolphins like swimming with their family?

Yes, they do.

2 Where do dolphins swim?

3 Are all sharks big?

4 What color are sharks?

10 **Read the text and choose the best answer.** 📖 ✏️

1 Mother polar bear:

"How are you this morning?"

Cub: **a** "I am very well."

   b "I am playing."

2 Mother elephant:

"Would you like to drink some water?"

Calf: **a** "No, it is not."

   b "Yes, please."

3 Mother cheetah:

"Did your brother play with you?"

Cub: **a** "Yes, he did."

   b "Yes, I did."

4 Mother gibbon:

"Are you hungry?"

Father: **a** "Yes, I am!"

   b "No, we cannot."

11 **Look and read.**
Put a ✓ or a ✗ in the box.

1 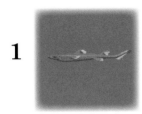 This is a shark.

2 These are scorpions.

3 Fennec foxes
live here.

4  Dolphins live
in groups.

5  This is a little shark.

12 Write the missing letters.

r r   c h   b b   p h   p h

1  e l e **p h** a n t

2  d o l ＿ ＿ i n

3  ＿ ＿ e e t a h

4  g i ＿ ＿ o n

5  p a ＿ ＿ o t

13 Read the questions and answers.
Write *Why*, *What*, or *When*. 📖 ✏️

1 ___When___ did the elephants
drink some water?

They drank some water in
the morning.

2 _____ did the cheetah
cub run across the plains?

It was frightened.

3 _____ did the gibbons
see in the trees?

They saw some parrots.

4 _____ did the parrots
go to sleep?

They went to sleep at night.

14 **Match the pictures to the sentences.**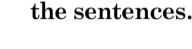

1

a This animal is brown and goes from tree to tree.

2

b This animal can run very fast.

3

c This animal lives in the desert. It has got big ears.

4

d This animal lives in the jungle in big and little groups.

5

e This animal is small. It helps its little children.

15 **Ask and answer the questions with a friend.** 💬

1

> What is your favorite wild animal? Why?

> My favorite wild animal is the fennec fox because it has got big ears.

2 Would you like to see an elephant with its calf?

3 Where do people see wild animals today?

4 Do you like scorpions? Why? Why not?

5 Would you like to go to the Arctic and see polar bears? Why? Why not?

16 **Ask and answer questions about the picture with a friend.**

Sharks

There are a lot of sharks in the sea.

Some are big and some are little.

26

Example:

Where do sharks live?

They live in the sea.

17 Look at the pictures. Write the answers. 📖 ✏️

1 How many cubs has the fennec fox got?

The fennec fox has got
four cubs.

2 How many cubs has the polar bear got?

....

....

3 Which calves swim in the sea?

....

....

18 **Circle the names of five wild animals.**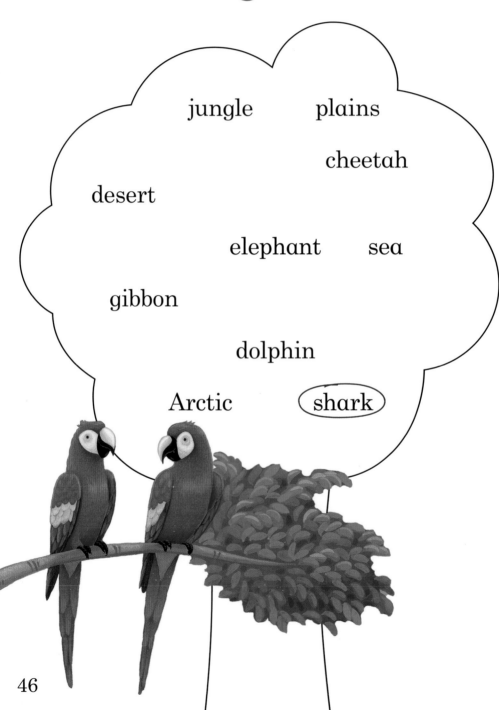

jungle   plains

cheetah

desert

elephant   sea

gibbon

dolphin

Arctic   shark

19 **Read the text and circle the best answer.**

1 The Arctic is very ....
   a cold.
   b hot.

2 Baby elephants are called

   ....

   a cubs.
   b calves.

3 Cheetahs run across the

   ....

   a desert.
   b plains.

4 Gibbons live in family groups in the

   ....

   a jungle.
   b desert.

Level 2

Level 2
The Gingerbread
Man

978–0–241–25442–4

Level 2
Sly Fox and
Red Hen

978–0–241–25443–1

Level 2
The Monster
Next Door

978–0–241–25444–8

Level 2
Wild Animals

978–0–241–25445–5

Level 2
Little Red
Riding Hood

978–0–241–25446–2

Level 2
Dinosaurs

978–0–241–25447–9

Level 2
Topsy and Tim
The Big Race

978–0–241–25448–6

Level 2
Peter Rabbit Goes
to the Treehouse

978–0–241–25449–3

Level 2
Sports Day

978–0–241–26222–1

Level 2
Going on a Picnic

978–0–241–26221–4

Now you're ready for Level 3!

Notes
CEFR levels are based on guidelines set out in the Council
of Europe's European Framework. Cambridge Young Learners
English (YLE) Exams give a reliable indication of a child's
progression in learning English.